Communication Skills For Product Managers

The Communication Skills That Product Managers Need To Know How To Use In Order To Have A Successful Product

"Practical, proven communication techniques that will help you to have a successful product manager career"

Dr. Jim Anderson

Published by:
Blue Elephant Consulting
Tampa, Florida

Copyright © 2013 by Dr. Jim Anderson

All rights reserved. No part of this book may be reproduced of transmitted in any form or by any means, electronic or mechanical, including photocopying, recording or by any information storage and retrieval system without written permission of the publisher, except for inclusion of brief quotations in a review.

Printed in the United States of America

Library of Congress Control Number: 2013921352

ISBN-13: 978-1494207724
ISBN-10: 1494207729

Warning – Disclaimer

The purpose of this book is to educate and entertain. This book does not promise or guarantee that anyone following the ideas, tips, suggestions, techniques or strategies will be successful. The author, publisher and distributor(s) shall have neither liability nor responsibility to anyone with respect to any loss or damage caused, or alleged to be caused, directly or indirectly by the information contained in this book.

Other Books By The Author

Product Management

- How To Have A Successful Product Manager Career: The Things That You Need To Be Doing TODAY In Order To Have A Successful Product Manager Career

- Product Manager Product Success: How to keep your product on track and make it become a success

Public Speaking

- Secrets To Planning The Perfect Speech

- Secrets To Organizing The Perfect Speech: How to organize the best speech of your life!

CIO Skills

- CIO Business Skills: How CIOs can work effectively with the rest of the company!

- Managing Your CIO Career: Steps That CIOs Have To Take In Order To Have A Long And Successful Career

IT Manager Skills

- IT Manager Budgeting Skills

- IT Manager Career Secrets: Tips And Techniques That IT Managers Can Use In Order To Have A Successful Career

Negotiating

- Preparing For Your Next Negotiation: What You Need To Do BEFORE A Negotiation Starts In Order To Get The Best Possible Deal

- How To Open Your Next Negotiation: How To Start A Negotiation In Order To Get The Best Possible Outcome

Miscellaneous

- Power Distribution Unit (PDU) Secrets: What Everyone Who Works In A Data Center Needs To Know!

- Making The Jump: How To Land Your Dream Job When You Get Out Of College!

Acknowledgements

Any book like this one is the result of years of real-world work experience. In my over 25 years of working for 7 different firms, I have met countless fantastic people and I've been mentored by some truly exceptional ones. Although I've probably forgotten some of the people who made me the person that I am today, here is my attempt to finally give them the recognition that they so truly deserve:

- Thomas P. Anderson
- Art Puett
- Bobbi Marshall
- Bob Boggs

Dr. Jim Anderson

This book is dedicated to my wife Lori. None of this would have been possible without her love and support.

Thanks for the best 21 years of my life (so far)...!

Table Of Contents

WHAT'S THE BIG DEAL ABOUT COMMUNICATION SKILLS? 8

ABOUT THE AUTHOR 10

CHAPTER 1: THE BEST WAY TO COMMUNICATE IS... 14

CHAPTER 2: GOT A MINUTE? THE POWER OF MEETING MINUTES ...17

CHAPTER 3: FACE-TO-FACE MEETINGS: ONLINE VS. OFFLINE? 20

CHAPTER 4: PRODUCT MANAGER ALERT: DEALING WITH HARD CORE OPPOSITION WITHIN YOUR COMPANY 23

CHAPTER 5: BRAINSTORMING: HOW TO DO IT THE RIGHT WAY! 27

CHAPTER 6: THE SECRET TO SUCCESSFUL PRODUCT MANAGEMENT IS 31

CHAPTER 7: WOULD YOU LIKE TO SHARE MY PURPOSE? 34

CHAPTER 8: PRODUCT MANAGER WHAT DOES YOUR BUSINESS CARD SAY ABOUT YOU? 37

CHAPTER 9: HOW QUICKLY DO PRODUCT MANAGERS NEED TO REACT TO BAD PRESS ABOUT THEIR PRODUCT? 41

CHAPTER 10: #1 SECRET WEAPON OF A SUCCESSFUL PRODUCT MANAGER 45

CHAPTER 11: PRODUCT MANAGER SECRETS FOR DEALING WITH EMAIL 49

CHAPTER 12: PRODUCT MANAGER TIPS: HOW TO USE SUBLIMINAL ADVERTISING 52

What's The Big Deal About Communication Skills?

Do product managers have super powers? Probably not, but there are some product managers who seem to be more successful than others. These "super" product managers seem to be able to make things happen almost effortlessly. What's their secret?

More often than not, when you take a look at how super product managers go about doing their job, you'll quickly discover that they are great communicators. This means that they are able to express their thoughts clearly and get others to quickly understand what they need to have done.

The rest of us can learn a lot from these super product managers. What we need to learn is how to improve our communication skills. Oh sure, we already have communication skills; however, we could always use a little help in making them better.

One of the most important places that a product manager needs to be a good communicator is in business meetings. So much of what affects our product happens in meetings that knowing how to make the most of face-to-face and online meetings is a key part of the product management job. We also have to know how to make sure that that actions that come out of meetings actually get followed up on.

The job of a product manager revolves around communicating with large numbers of different people. This means that we need to know when we should use the phone, email, or face-to-face contact in order to get what we need to have done, done.

Contained in this book are the tips and tricks that you are going to need in order to become a more effect communicator. As you read each chapter, take a moment to think about how you can start to use the information in your job immediately. I think that you are going to be both surprised and pleased with just how much this information is going to help you to clearly communicate what you need others to do for you!

For more information on what it takes to be a great product manager, check out my blog, The Accidental Product Manager, at:

www.TheAccidentalPM.com

Good luck!

- Dr. Jim Anderson, November, 2013

About The Author

I must confess that I never set out to be a product manager. When I went to school, I studied Computer Science and thought that I'd get a nice job programming and that would be that. Well, at least part of that plan worked out!

My first job was working for Boeing on their F/A-18 fighter jet program. I spent my days programming fighter jet software in assembly language and I loved it. The U.S. government decided to save some money and went looking for other countries to sell this plane to. This put me into an unfamiliar role: I started to meet with foreign military officials in order to explain what my product did.

Time moved on and so did I. I found myself working for Siemens, the big German telecommunications company. They were making phone switches and selling them to the seven U.S. phone companies. The problem was that the switches were too complicated. Customers couldn't tell the difference between one complicated phone switch from another complicated phone switch.

The Siemens sales folks were in a bind. They didn't know enough about how the switches worked to tell their customers why they should buy them. Siemens reached out into their engineering unit looking for anyone who could help the sales teams out. I put my hand up and overnight I became a product manager.

Since then I've spent over 20 years working as a product manager for both big companies and startups. This has given me an opportunity to do everything that a product manager does many, many times. I know what works as well as what doesn't work.

I now live in Tampa Florida where I spend my time managing my consulting business, Blue Elephant Consulting, teaching college courses at the University of South Florida, and traveling to work with companies like yours to share the knowledge that I have about how product managers can make their product be a success.

I'm always available to answer questions and I can be reached at:

Dr. Jim Anderson
Blue Elephant Consulting
Email: jim@BlueElephantConsulting.com
Facebook: http://goo.gl/1TVoK
Web: http://www.BlueElephantConsulting.com/

"Unforgettable communication skills that will set your ideas free..."

Create Products Your Customers Want At A Price That They Are Willing To Pay!

Dr. Jim Anderson is available to provide training and coaching on the two topics that are the most important to product managers everywhere: how do I create the products that my customers want and what should I price them at?

Dr. Anderson believes that in order to both learn and remember what he says, product managers need to laugh. Each one of his speeches is full of fun and humor so that what he says "sticks" with everyone.

Dr. Anderson's Product Management Training Includes:

1. How can you segment your market?
2. What problems are your customers having right now?
3. Which of your customer's problems does your product solve?
4. How much of this problem does your product solve?
5. How much will it cost your customer if they don't fix this problem?

Dr. Jim Anderson presents over 100 speeches per year. To invite Dr. Anderson to speak at your event, contact him at:

Phone: 813-418-6970 or
Email: jim@BlueElephantConsulting.com

Blue Elephant Consulting

Speaking. Negotiating. Managing. Marketing.

Chapter 1

The Best Way To Communicate Is...

Chapter 1: The Best Way To Communicate Is...

Here in the comfortable 21st Century, product managers have many different ways to communicate with their boss/team/etc. However, just because you have a lot of ways to say something, does not mean that you are using the correct way to say it.

Email is our favorite (ok, how about most used?) communication tool. We get emails, we read emails, we send emails. The problem is that it is all too easy to view email as our only communication channel. We've got others:

1. Email
2. Instant Messaging
3. Phone
4. Written Note
5. Physical Visit

Both emails and IM messages suffer from a key failure: they lack any way to communicate emotion. "Come to my office" is a message that, depending on the emotion with which it is delivered, can have many different meetings.

Let me wrap this discussion up with a true story that will help me make my point. One Friday afternoon (these things always happen on Fridays) I got a call from my product's development team leader. He told me that the feature that a VP had requested be added to the next release of the product would not be making it into the product because his team did not have any requirements.

I thanked him for the head's up. Hung up the phone and briefly considered how short my career was going to be once the VP discovered that we had apparently ignored his request. I then called the requirements team and asked if they had requirements for this feature.

Their team lead told me that they couldn't start working on those requirements until they got funding to do so. I then called the folks in finance and asked if funding was available. They said "sure, just tell us where it needs to go."

A quick call back to requirements confirmed that they could have the requirements done by the end of the day once funding was confirmed. A final call to development secured me an assurance that the coding would be done by the end of the weekend if the requirements were available by the end of the day. Whew — problem solved.

The take-away here is that the phone calls were the key. Everyone had already been sending emails about this issue, but that had not solved the problem. It's the small things that make someone an effective product manager.

Chapter 2

Got A Minute? The Power Of Meeting Minutes

Chapter 2: Got A Minute? The Power Of Meeting Minutes

The difference between an effective product manager and an ineffective product manager often comes down to the little things. One big "little thing" is how you deal with meeting minutes.

It was years ago when I was up to my neck in standards bodies work for the ATM protocol, a participant who was much wiser than I was took me aside and informed me that whoever had the role of secretary had the most power in the process.

When I asked why, he explained that nobody could ever remember what was talked about during the meeting and whatever came out later in the minutes was always treated as fact no matter what was actually said.

This is a powerful truth that has ramifications in the world of Product Managers. In all of the face-to-face meetings and phone conferences that we participate in quickly blur together as we move through the week.

All too often folks seem to repeat themselves meeting after meeting going over issues that have already been discussed. This is simply because nobody remembers what was discussed or agreed to in past meetings.

Sometimes meeting minutes are produced; however, they are generally hard to read/use and quickly discarded. Consistency is the key to long term minute success. If you want to be an effective product manager, then you need to grab the meeting minute bull by the horns and become the source of minutes for all of your meetings and calls.

What makes good meeting minutes? The #1 thing that readers are looking for is how they are impacted by the minutes. This means that you should quickly document what the meeting was about and when it was held.

Then after that you need to list the actions that came out from the meeting. Each action need to contain three things: what needs to be done, who needs to do it, and when it needs to be completed. Here's what an action should look like:

> 1. **Action**: Investigate why warp engine continues to malfunction during light speed jumps.
> **Assigned**: Hans Solo, Due: 07/04/08

A small important point is that actions should be grouped by who they are assigned to (all of Hans' actions should be listed one after another). If during a meeting important conclusions were reached, then this should be listed BEFORE the actions. These should look like:

> 1. **Conclusion**: It was agreed by all that the Empire should be overthrown as quickly as possible.

This will always be a short list and listing it before the actions means that everyone will look at it before they go searching for actions that have their name assigned to them.

Remember the famous saying: "History is written by the winners." The same thing can be said about product management meetings, minutes and actions!

Chapter 3

Face-To-Face Meetings: Online vs. Offline?

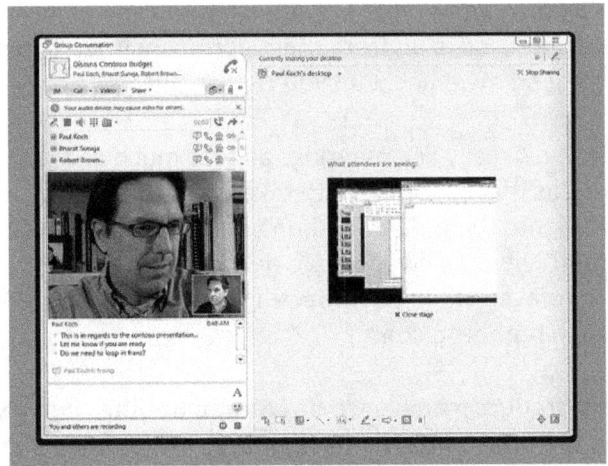

Chapter 3: Face-To-Face Meetings: Online vs. Offline?

How many of you have seen this: you've called a technical face to face meeting to resolve some key product issues. You've carefully coordinated the meeting time with everyone's schedules and you've been sure to make sure that you've included folks from all impacted departments.

Imagine your joy when you see that just about everyone has actually shown up for your meeting. Imagine your disappointment when everyone whips out their laptops, powers up. gets a wired/wireless connection, and *poof* they mentally vanish.

So why are we having this meeting? I can't tell you how many times I've been in one of these meetings when someone gets asked a question, looks up from their laptop and says "I'm sorry, I was working on my email. Can you repeat the question?"

I generally don't really like meetings all that much and it's events like this that cause them to take way too long. If you introduce IM into the equation, then you have folks in your meeting merrily typing away in one or more active conversations even while your meeting is going on. Arrgh! Why did they even bother to come?

So what's a product manager to do? Stomping your feet, rolling around on the floor, and shaking your finger at offenders are all possibilities; however, I'm not thinking that they will really accomplish the goal. What is the goal? To have a face-to-face meeting with all parties attending participating and engaged in the conversation and problem solving.

This is a huge problem and we have yet to really work out the social issues that it brings up. For example, if your boss attends and opens his/her laptop, then what are you going to say to him/her?

I don't have any magic solutions, but one powerful force that you can bring to bear is peer pressure. If before the meeting occurs you loudly and clearly tell everyone that the use of laptops and Blackberrys will be banned during the meeting, then nobody can really object.

If you hold the line and actually kick out active Blackberry users that will also send a clear message. Careful though — if they don't leave, then you will have lost face with the rest of the attendees. Finally, make you meetings exciting and engaging. People do other tasks because they are bored. If you remove the boredom, they may even forget about their laptops/Blackberrys/iPhones for at least awhile.

Chapter 4

Product Manager Alert: Dealing With Hard Core Opposition Within Your Company

Chapter 4: Product Manager Alert: Dealing With Hard Core Opposition Within Your Company

We've talked about why Product Managers find it hard to get any respect. Now it's time to talk about the why's and how's of what to do when you run into another department (or person) who acts like a brick wall.

Thanks to millions of years of evolution, we are all pretty good at recognizing situations in which we are called on to compete with other departments who are willing to do business with us. We are tuned to allow us to make ourselves heard in these situations and to get our point across. Which is why we all seem to do such a poor job when we are faced with not competition, but rather opposition. Oh, oh. What to do now?

So what is opposition? Opposition is what happens when the group of people that you are trying to communicate with are just dead set against what you have to say. This is not unique to Product Management — a Project Manager can have exactly the same problem.

If you show up in a situation where you are going to be telling your team about a great new product that the company has decided to start developing, you will encounter opposition if nobody that you are talking to wants to work on that product in the first place — it's not that the new product is a bad idea (although it might be), it's just that everyone rejects the idea of working on that product.

What's funny is that although in technical fields we struggle with how to deal with opposition, the folks who work in politics deal with it on a daily basis. Our elected officials are forced to deal with opposition every day and so they have developed effective ways of dealing with it. We could learn a thing or two from them:

- **Co-opt The Other Side's Issue**: this is one of my favorite approaches. Don't go head-to-head with the opposition. Instead take a careful look at what's motivating their position: why doesn't the other department want to work on your product?

    If you show respect for their underlying issue and then go ahead and propose a different way of solving it, you'll basically cut off the opposition at the knees. In our product case, if you show the team that offshore developers do a poor job of creating products when there is minimal documentation and by doing a good job of development their work they will be able to keep more jobs onshore, then you've accomplished your co-opting.

- **Redefine The Issue**: Initially an issue may start out as a tug-of-war. In order to solve this problem, if you redefine it in such a way that it is no longer a tug-of-war, then you can win the other side over.

    In our product example, the issue could start out as a "the company is telling us to do more work". This could be redefined as "Other companies have created products that interface with our product. In order for them (and us) to be successful, we have to extend the interfaces that they are using to connect to our product." All of a sudden, what was something that was being created for the faceless company becomes a tool for specific small business owners.

If you can become skilled at learning to distinguish opposition from competition, then you will have a hard-to-find skill that you can start to use proactively. Do a little bit of research on the department that you will be communicating with. If there is strong opposition to what you will be discussing with them, it will probably come out quickly. Look for ways to co-opt or redefine the issue and you'll have accomplished half of your job before you even open your mouth.

Chapter 5

Brainstorming: How To Do It The Right Way!

Chapter 5: Brainstorming: How To Do It The Right Way!

If you've even come close to a business book in the last 5 years or so, you have probably discovered that "innovation" is what every marketing organization is desperately trying to capture, grow, encourage, enhance, etc. Although this sounds like a great idea, and product management is one area that would directly benefit from this, it turns out that it's actually quite hard to do consistently over time. What gives?

One of the key skills that a organization needs in order to be innovative and to develop better products, is the ability to brainstorm as a team well. We all THINK that we know what it means to brainstorm; however, it turns out that more often than not we are wrong.

Too often we think of brainstorming as being a solitary task where we go off an think about a problem until an apple drops on our head and the answer emerges. Matt Bowen who is the CEO of Aloft Group spends a lot of time teaching his marketing firm's employees how to brainstorm as a group — a much more powerful form of brainstorming. Here are his suggestions for how you can learn to use this powerful tool:

- **Creativity Starts With The Hiring Process**: When you are inviting people to join your team, you need to make sure that they will be able to contribute to the group's ability to innovate. This means that you need to understand how they think.

    A great way to do this is to ask them to tell you stories about jobs that they've had. If their stories revolve around creating new solutions than you know that you have a creative type. If instead, they focus on incremental improvements in the way that things are done, then you're probably talking with an operations person.

- **How To Prepare To Brainstorm In A Group**: The best way to learn to do this is to jump in and just do it. You will need to have a designated facilitator to lead the process.

    The first thing that the facilitator needs to help the group do is to very clearly lay out a single sentence that clearly describes what the goal of the brainstorming session is. Distribute this sentence a day or two before the meeting to everyone who will be attending so that they can start to think about it.

    Also, the facilitator needs to spend some time establishing criteria for how he/she thinks the resulting ideas need to be rated. What are the most important characteristics of a solution and how should you rank them?

- **Group Brainstorming Rules**: Never have the meeting last more than an hour. Limit the size of the meeting to no more than 5-7 people (less if the facilitator is new to this).

    Try to make sure that the participants come from different departments because this will help to ensure that you get multiple perspectives. Normal brainstorming rules apply: no critiquing, no editing, no such thing as a bad idea, and always try to build on other people's ideas.

The real key to successful brainstorming lies in what you do AFTER the meeting. The facilitator needs to assemble a group of people to rate the ideas generated by the brainstorming based on the criteria that was established before the meeting. This group can be different from the group that created the ideas.

Finally, don't you let the resulting ideas die! In order for brainstorming to catch on in any department the staff need to see changes occurring that they can clearly relate back to brainstorming sessions. Do this and you'll have an innovative department that will be the envy of the rest of the firm.

Chapter 6

The Secret To Successful Product Management Is

...

Chapter 6: The Secret To Successful Product Management Is ...

... leadership. Sorry in advance for this rant, but I've just about had it with product managers who spent their time whining and complaining that nobody listens to them. Pretty much across the board I've seem organizations where IT Product Managers get less respect than Rodney Dangerfield (on a good day!).

In talking with these Product Managers, I think that I've heard just about every excuse that you could imagine: "it's really an engineering company and I'm not an engineer", "they don't work well with women", "most of the team is in India and they think differently", "this is a low priority project", etc. To which I say, just shut up already. The time for Product Managers to feeling sorry for themselves is over – nobody has time to listen to them anymore.

What's wrong with all of these complaints? The accusing finger of blame is pointing in the wrong direction: it's not everyone else's fault, it's the Product Manager's fault. Yes — I'm blaming the Product Manager, get over it. We really have done a lousy job of clearly defining who we are, what the qualifications to be Product Manager are, and just exactly what value we bring to the company. Who can blame everyone else for not respecting us?

What's Wrong With Product Managers?
Most (98%) of Product Managers don't understand the #1 rule of being a Product Manager: you are the CEO of your product. I really don't care if anyone told you that you were (normally they don't); however, they sure are going to hold you responsible if it fails so you may as well grab the reigns and start to drive that product wagon because if you don't, then nobody else will.

A good 75% of Product Managers then go on to mess up Rule #2 of being a Product Manager: it's all about the people. Do you know what the difference between a project manager and a Product Manager is? Scope.

A project manager has a clear start and finish to a project and gets to lose him/herself in tracking the progress of that project. A Product Manager operates on a higher plane and needs to ensure that the world is ready for the product once the project manager is done. Oh, and that the product that was created was the right product with the right features.

What To Do?

So what is a Product Manager to do? Let's keep this nice and simple — show some leadership. A Product Manager can't "manage" because nobody works for them. Instead, a Product Manager needs to inspire those that he/she works with in order to have them work on those items that the Product Manager needs to have done.

IT staff, finance staff, marketing folks, etc. all need to come together and do work at the request of a Product Manager for whom they do not actually work. The only way that this can be done successfully is for the Product Manager to set an example of leadership by showing the team the correct way forward. This means that the Product Manager needs to have great interpersonal skills, lots of time and patience, and the ability to simplify complex product status in order to communicate it to many different parties.

How hard can this be? It turns out that it is very hard. There are lots of different Product Management courses out there; however, there is precious few courses on Product Management leadership. Maybe it's time that Leadership becomes the new focus for all Product Managers...

Chapter 7

Would You Like To Share My Purpose?

Chapter 7: Would You Like To Share My Purpose?

One of the key differences between a product manager and a project manager is that a product manager truly needs to motivate others to do work for him/her. A project manager can get away with just reporting on the current status of a project, a product manager needs to make that product successful.

High-commitment, high-performance (HCHP) product management leaders realize this and have come to realize that they won't be able to be successful unless they can find a way to create a purpose that can be shared across the entire product team.

As our product teams spread out farther and farther across the globe, our ability to create this sense of shared purpose become even more difficult. Product teams that are successful have to share more than just a common employer.

Product managers have to spend a lot of time, energy, and effort in creating a shared purpose that will have an emotional appeal to each member of the team. This can go a long way in developing an entrepreneurial spirit within the team. How's that for a real soft skill? Every successful shared purpose has the same three components:

- it allows the employees to create a better world in which to live in,

- it allows them to deliver performance that they can all be proud of, and

- by subscribing to it they will be able to be in an environment in which they can personally grow.

Each component of this type of shared purpose both helps the firm as well as acting as a powerful motivation tool for the employees working on the product.

Creating a better world in which to live in. Although we may all be working together on a product, what are we doing to improve the world in which we live in? This can take several different forms. Doing work in the community as a team, collecting funds to help people in remote areas, etc. all allow the team to pull together on an issue that is outside of work. However, this bonding then spills over and ties the team together more closely.

Deliver performance that they can be proud of. If the product team is not being recognized as a high performance team, then the people working on that team won't be getting fulfillment from participating. At the end of the day, the best workers really want to work with the other best workers. If it is at all possible for a product manager to choose who works on their product, then by all means select only the best workers. If not, then you need to find ways to get peak performance out of your team.

Be in an environment in which they can personally grow. Ultimately we all want to have an opportunity to reach our own personal peak potential. The only way to do this is to ensure that the job of every person who is working on the product is both personally fulfilling and one that they can get excited about. What this means for a product manager is that you need to be constantly be working to ensure that everyone on the product team is being challenged and has opportunities to grow.

Chapter 8

Product Manager What Does Your Business Card Say About You?

Chapter 8: Product Manager What Does Your Business Card Say About You?

So here's a minor topic that might have some real significance for all product managers: what do you put on your business card? Yeah, yeah, I know that we're living in the age of FaceBook and LinkedIn but business cards are still what we exchange when we meet people face-to-face. What this means is that business cards still matter. What's on your business card?

At this point in my career I must have had no less than 20 different business cards. Every once in a while I'll see a collection of them huddled together in the bottom of some drawer somewhere and I'll have to smile as I realize just how much my description of myself and what I do has changed over time.

I'll never forget when I got my first opportunity to sign up for business cards. This was it, I had made the big time. Despite being a lowly software engineer now I was finally going to have an "adult" way to communicate to others just how important I was. As with all large firms, most of the format of the business card was pre-established. However, I was given free rein to add my job title just under my name. Hmm, what to put? The first time out of the gate I put what the company listed for me in the corporate directory: "Software Engineer IV" or whatever.

It turns out that this was a big mistake. Outside of people who worked for my company, nobody else in the real world knew what a Software Engineer IV was! I'd get polite smiles and then the card would quickly disappear into someone's pocket to probably be thrown away when it came time to do laundry.

A few business card iterations later, I started to get smarter. By this time I had moved over into the world of Product Management and so I changed my job title to "Product

Manager". This was much better. I don't think very many people knew what a Product Manager was or did, but they sure thought that they knew what a manager did and so upon receiving my card they slotted me as a mid-level manager and left it at that.

The promotions came over time and whereas I was not yet a Vice President or a CIO yet, I had become a Senior Product Manager. At the next opportunity I updated the business card title to read "Senior Product Manager". This seemed to garner me just a little bit more respect when I handed the card out. Once again, I don't think that very many people knew what I did; however, they seemed to believe that I was now in the upper echelons of mid-level managers.

I was still finding that since folks didn't actually know what a Product Manager does, they were struggling to pigeonhole me based on my title. The trick here is that if people can't figure out quickly where you fit in the totem pole of responsibility, then they will end up not even bothering to try.

I felt that one more evolution was required. I ended up dropping the "Product" and so today my business card reads simply "Senior Manager". Although less descriptive, I've found this title to be of great use at trade shows and when meeting with vendors.

No, they still really don't seem to know what I do for the company; however, they are easily able to realize that a "Senior Manager" is someone who must be very important. This means that they treat me as being someone important because they don't have any reason not to.

One final note, with my obtuse title the very first question that I get asked is "what do you do?" This is a make-or-break question. If I identify myself as a Product Manager, this will get me classified as a low-level worker bee because nobody really knows what a Product Manager does. Over countless encounters like this I have honed my response to reply with a quick "I make problems go away." In most cases, this generates quiet respect and there are no more probing questions.

Chapter 9

How Quickly Do Product Managers Need To React To Bad Press About Their Product?

Chapter 9: How Quickly Do Product Managers Need To React To Bad Press About Their Product?

There is a saying that goes "Any publicity is good publicity". It turns out that this is wrong. In fact, after having given birth to or adopting a product, a Product Manager can see the good name of their product vanish almost overnight if they aren't careful.

A good example of this, on a very large scale, is what happened to United Airlines back in September. Way back in 2002 United's parent company, UAL, had been forced to file bankruptcy. They had worked their way out of this and it was old news. Until an old article talking about the bankruptcy filing showed up on Google's news service as apparently new news.

What had happened is that Google's information gathering technology which cruises the web each evening found a new link on the South Florida Sun-Sentinel newspaper's web site. The article didn't carry a date but it had been originally published by the Chicago Tribune back in December of 2002. The article had not been there the last time Google's crawler had visited the Sun-Sentinel's site and so it was flagged this time as new news.

How this old story had appeared on the Sun-Sentinel's business news section was originally unclear. However, it is now believed that because of bad weather in south Florida, people had been checking the news about travel delays and enough of them may have stumbled onto the old UAL story by mistake to cause it to be promoted to a high position on the Sun-Sentinel's list of news stories.

As you can well imagine there are a lot of people who subscribe to services that automatically alert them to any news about UAL. When this new/old story hit Google's wire, lots of people got an email that told them that UAL had just filed for bankruptcy (remember, there had been no date associated with the original story). Next, stock market research firms picked up the story and finally it hit the Bloomberg financial news service whose stories are treated as gospel. In 15 minutes UAL shares dropped down to $3/share. Poof – there went UAL's product.

What does all of this mean to a product manager? In the bold new world of the 21st Century your product's reputation can be lost literally overnight if you are not careful. Rightly or wrongly the Internet and the army of automated news collectors and automatic stock trading programs can work together to pummel your product and your firm quicker than you can catch your breath. This is the time for all of us to become good Boy Scouts and "Be Prepared".

Realizing that an event like this can happen to your product is the first step in preparing a reaction plan. The next step is to assume the worst has happened: bad press about your product has hit the wire. What would you do? The correct response is probably to create a press release, post something prominently on your firm's web site, and make senior executives available for interviews with the press in order to provide the company's view on whatever event is being reported.

Instead of running around like a chicken with your head cut off when a bad press event like this happens, why not prepare right now? How much of that press release could you write today? Who would have to review and approve it before it could be released? Do you have their contact info?

If you needed to have your web site updated in a hurry, who would do that and would they be available no matter what time of day the update was needed? What members of the press could you get your senior executives in contact with quickly? What have you already done to make them friendly (or at least neutral) towards your company?

All of these are activities that can save your skin and your product in the event of bad press poisoning the well of potential customers that you hope to drink from. Do some work now and you just might save your job later...!

Chapter 10

#1 Secret Weapon Of A Successful Product Manager

Chapter 10: #1 Secret Weapon Of A Successful Product Manager

Being a Product Manager is hard work, being a successful product manager is even harder. Wouldn't we all like to have a secret weapon that would allow us to cut through all of the roadblocks that others seem to be constantly throwing up all around us?

Just imagine if there was some way to get everyone to actually do what they have promised that they would do. Wouldn't that at least be a step in the right direction? We've talked in the past about other powerful tools that all product managers have at their disposal, but I've been saving the best for now.

It is a simple and perhaps sad fact of modern business life that nobody (including you) has enough time to get everything done anymore. What this means is that actions that people agreed to do during meetings, requests that you've made, and pleas that you've sent via email will probably mostly get ignored.

Yes, there is a possibility that people aren't doing what you need them to do because they don't like you. However, to not like someone takes energy so it's more likely that people are probably blowing you off because they've got too much other higher priority work that needs to be done. Sorry, you lose.

This should be a big deal to you. The modern product manager really does not create anything – instead we work with and through others to get things done. Our dirty little secret is that nobody works for us and so we really don't have any authority to demand that things get done. Instead, we can only ask. That phrase "**all the responsibility, none of the authority**" was really created for us.

It's almost enough to make a hard working product manager throw his/her hands up in the air and give up. But wait – before you do that, I've got good news for you – there is a secret weapon that you can use to make your life better.

This secret weapon is called "the follow-up". No, wait – don't stop reading now! Trust me on this one, the follow-up has the ability to change your life (I know this because it changed my life). The reason that I like to call this a secret weapon is because amazingly enough it really does seem to be a secret – almost nobody else is using it!

Here's a typical scenario that this secret weapon can come into play in: you attend a meeting, a discussion occurs, actions are created and assigned, the meeting is over and everyone leaves. All too often, that's it – nobody ever follows up on those actions. This means that the same topics will be revisited in another meeting, more actions will be assigned, and those actions won't be followed-up on either. And so on, and so on.

As a product manager with your new follow-up secret weapon, you can take charge of the actions that you care about. Make sure that each of them has a clear owner before the meeting breaks up. Also make sure that each action has an associated due date. Once this is done, you need to make yourself a "follow-up checklist".

This checklist will tell you who you need to hound in order to make sure that they complete their actions on time. This list will grow once you start including outstanding emails on it. How many times have you sent an email with a question to someone and then forgotten about it (and they have too!)? Not any more, now when you send that email w/ a question, add it to your follow-up checklist.

What's going to happen is very quickly you are going to take on the demeanor of a bulldog in your work environment. People are going to start to realize that when you are promised information, you are not going to let up until you get it. This means that the people who owe you info will move it up their priority list.

Yes, I know that this sounds like a very simple secret weapon; however, its power is not to be underestimated. Give it a try and I think that you'll be pleased with the results.

Chapter 11

Product Manager Secrets For Dealing With Email

Chapter 11: Product Manager Secrets For Dealing With Email

So here we stand together filled with hopes and dreams that this year will be better than last. Now if we could just do something about that email problem that we've all been dealing with...

I don't know about you, but depending on what part of the product development / release cycle I'm currently at, I can get up to about 300 emails a day. Talk about a Tsunami! You may have already guessed that not all of those emails are all that important; however, I still need to work my way through the pile in order to find the ones that are important!

In the past I was just overwhelmed by this amount of email. I'd sit down and try to work my way through the pile, but by the time I got a few answered, more would have arrived! There seemed to be no way to climb this mountain.

Desperate for some sort of solution, I looked around for a solution. Based on some blogs that I had read, I discovered David Allen's Getting Things Done approach. I read his book and spent some time thinking about what he had to say.

I must confess that there were a lot of things that David suggested doing that I was just unable to put into practice in my life for one reason or another. However, he made some really good points about email that struck home with me.

David basically said that too many of us (me included) tend to use our "inbox" as a storage place for emails. His suggestion was that we clean out our inboxes and keep them clean. Hmm, this sure seemed like just the thing that I needed to do.

At work I use the corporate Microsoft Exchange email system. After reading David's book, I went ahead and created two new folders to store email in. I called these folders "@Action" and "@Waiting For". The "@" symbol is used to make both of these folders easy to find by having them show up at the top of my list of Outlook folders.

The "@Action" folder is used to temporarily store emails that I need to look at further. This allows me to quickly step through my new emails and throw away the junk, reply to the quick answers, and file everything else in @Action.

This allows me to process immense amounts of email very quickly. Yes, I realize that this means that I've got more work to do, but it's still a step in the right direction. Words cannot describe the incredible feeling of satisfaction that one feels when you see an empty email inbox!

The "@Waiting For" file is used slightly differently. Whenever I send an email to someone asking for information or requesting something, the challenge is to remember that I've asked for something (and what I've asked for). I "BCC" myself on these emails and when I get a copy of the email that I've sent, then I go ahead and file it in my "@Waiting For" file.

Now dear reader, you may have already spotted the one flaw in my clever system: I need to remember to review the "@Action" in order to work through those emails that require some study. I also have to remember to go through the "@Waiting For" file in order to go back and remind people that they owe me information.

No system is perfect, but this way of dealing with email has served me well for about 5 years now. I may find a better way in the future, but for now this one takes care of me.

Chapter 12

Product Manager Tips: How To Use Subliminal Advertising

Chapter 12: Product Manager Tips: How To Use Subliminal Advertising

Gosh – doesn't the whole concept of subliminal advertising just sound naughty to you? I mean, I've always sorts lumped this type of advertising together with hypnotism and sorta figured that they were slightly immoral. You know, it can't be right to get people to do things that they wouldn't do otherwise, right?

Let's assume that you are not trying to get your customers to take off their clothes (you are growing sleeeeepy...) or stop smoking or anything like that. Instead, you'd really like them to think positively about your product or, gasp, even go ahead and buy it.

Advertising and its kissing cousin subliminal advertising are generally thought of most often in terms of business-to-consumer marketing efforts. However, there is absolutely no reason that this concept can't also be applied to business-to-business advertising, product brochures, etc. After all, businesses don't buy products, people do.

Lots of really smart people have spent much time studying the field of subliminal advertising. Among them is Martin Lindstrom who is an international marketing expert and the author of **Buyology: Truth and Lies About Why We Buy**. Bruce has a few thoughts for how we can incorporate subliminal advertising concepts into our next product brochure / slide deck / website / etc.

1. **Product Feel Matters – A Lot!:** Here in the 21st century, we can do amazing things when we manufacture a "real" product that people can hold in their hands. However, sometimes we are too clever even for ourselves. Bruce has done studies with consumers using two different TV remote controls. Both had identical

functionality; however, one weighed more than the other. The heavier one was always reported to be of a higher quality. Even if your product is nothing more than an application that comes on a CD, including a "heavy" user guide in the box can improve your customer's perception of the quality of your product. If your product can be downloaded off the web, you've got a real "perceived quality" issue that you are going to need to overcome.

2. **Rituals Rule!**: Stress, time limits, and the state of the global economy are all weighing on our customers minds. As our personal stress levels grow, we unconsciously start to seek out those rituals that are the most familiar and comforting to us. By including images and words in your product material that associate your product with those rituals, your product will become more appealing to your customers.

3. **Music Soothes The Savage Customer**: The power of music to influence customer's buying habits is well known in retail circles. That's why you'll hear music with a slower beat in grocery stores – slower music makes you move slower and thus gives you more time to shop and buy. In many business-to-business situations, you don't have a chance to include much music. However, when customers come to your site for a product presentation or to negotiate a contract, putting on the right tunes can make all the difference in the world.

4. **Customers Want Cachet In What They Buy**: Sometimes it's called "putting on airs", but no matter what anyone says we all like to think that by buying a product we will become special in some way. If the product is expensive, rare, hard to get, or uses some special magic, then we want that product all the more.

Just because we may be responsible for products that are sold to businesses does not mean that the subliminal advertising techniques that have been developed for the retail market can't be used by us. Now the trick will be to make sure that we use this new found advertising power responsibly...!

Create Products Your Customers Want At A Price That They Are Willing To Pay!

Dr. Jim Anderson is available to provide training and coaching on the two topics that are the most important to product managers everywhere: how do I create the products that my customers want and what should I price them at?

Dr. Anderson believes that in order to both learn and remember what he says, product managers need to laugh. Each one of his speeches is full of fun and humor so that what he says "sticks" with everyone.

Dr. Anderson's Product Management Training Includes:

6. How can you segment your market?
7. What problems are your customers having right now?
8. Which of your customer's problems does your product solve?
9. How much of this problem does your product solve?
10. How much will it cost your customer if they don't fix this problem?

Dr. Jim Anderson presents over 100 speeches per year. To invite Dr. Anderson to speak at your event, contact him at:

Phone: 813-418-6970 or
Email: jim@BlueElephantConsulting.com

Photo Credits:

Cover - By: Paul Shanks
http://www.flickr.com/photos/pshanks/

Chapter 1 - By: Tim G. Photography
http://www.flickr.com/photos/93095839@N08/

Chapter 2 - By: Egyptians Abroad for Development
http://www.flickr.com/photos/64782942@N06/

Chapter 3 - By: Mary
http://www.flickr.com/photos/marypcb/

Chapter 4 - By: Jon Gilbert
http://www.flickr.com/photos/jon_gilbert/

Chapter 5 - By: TIG Photos
http://www.flickr.com/photos/theimagegroup/

Chapter 6 - By: Jessica Lucia
http://www.flickr.com/photos/theloushe/

Chapter 7 - By: Michael
http://www.flickr.com/photos/godserv/

Chapter 8 - By: Ronald Heft
http://www.flickr.com/photos/cavemonkey50/

Chapter 9 - By: Dave Winer
http://www.flickr.com/photos/scriptingnews/

Chapter 10 - By: Jedimentat44
http://www.flickr.com/photos/jedimentat/

Chapter 11 - By: Keith Ramsey
http://www.flickr.com/photos/rmgimages/

Chapter 12 - By: Satish Krishnamurthy
http://www.flickr.com/photos/unlistedsightings/

www.ingramcontent.com/pod-product-compliance
Lightning Source LLC
Chambersburg PA
CBHW071818170526
45167CB00003B/1357